The Homesick Patrol

The Homesick Patrol

David Vancil

Viet Nam Generation, Inc. & Burning Cities Press

The following poems have appeared or are forthcoming in the magazines
listed below. Many of the previously published poems have been revised
since their first appearance. Over half of the poems in this book were
written exclusively for this volume. None has appeared in a previous col-
lection.

Ant Farm: "Crucifixes"
California State Poetry Quarterly: "Seeing is Believing"
Free Lunch: "Legend of Dracula" & "Two Sisters"
Gopherwood Review: "Buster Crabbe"
Lowlands Review: "After the Harvest" & "The Carnival Elephant's Burial"
    ("Carnival Elephant" reprinted by *Viet Nam Generation*)
New Laurel Review: "Cloud Cover"
New Mexico Humanities Review: "Outpatient Surgery"
Pegasus: "The Fatty Acid Shuffle"
RE: Artes Liberales: "The Chalk Drawing"
Viet Nam Generation: "The Homesick Patrol" & "Horror Movie"

Cover design by Steven Gomes. Woodcut by Cedar Nordbye.

White Noise No. 3

White Noise Poetry

David Connolly, *Lost in America* (No. 1)
Elliot Richamn, *Walk On, Trooper* (No. 2)
David Vancil, *The Homesick Patrol* (No. 3)
Gerald McCarthy, *Throwing the Headlines* (No.4)
Joe Amato, *Symptoms of a Finer Age* (No. 5)
M.L. Liebler, *Stripping the Adult Century Bare* (No. 6)
Dale Ritterbusch, *Lessons Learned* (No. 7)
Philip K. Jason, *The Separation: Poems* (No. 8)

Viet Nam Generation, Inc. & Burning Cities Press
18 Center Road, Woodbridge, CT 06525
203/387-6882; FAX: 203/389-6104
email: kalital@minerva.cis.yale.edu
SAN: 298-2412

For France Edward and Bernadine May Vancil
And to the memory of Joy Scantlebury

Contents

Vietnam

Just Like Fried Chicken

Memoirs of an Ex-Baseball Player

Memoirs of an Ex-Baseball Player

Goats could have climbed among the jagged cliffs
that hugged the outfield. Whenever a long one
made it out, there was no telling where it
would land, back in play for easy bases
or atop our Matterhorn, a home run.
Even if it did come wobbling in
at the end of a socket-wrenching throw,
the ump's probing thumb would find
the split that had spoiled the stitched white cowhide.
No one thought once to ask him behind
his padded mask for it as a keepsake.
Trail of hopefuls, we remained intent on
knocking them out of sight, planets aimed at
the sun, as far away as Switzerland.

Dance Recital of the Five-Year-Olds

As the arc lamps' brilliant glare overlaps them,
tiny dancers strain against their clumsy childhoods,
not yet in quest of grace, those women's breasts
and behinds and legs that men will look at and long
to have. For now they miss their cues, wandering
stage left when they should go right, no thought
in their heads of betraying these imperfections
of womanhood, for now simple, innocent buds
in sunlight. And each father in the dark hall,
camera held to his eye, zooms in on her alone,
perfection personified, oblivious to goofs, flashing
pictures, making movies, art of a sort, wanting
to keep her new and whole, to know
her always as she is then, before like a close-up
her dance dissolves into another and leaves
only glimmering memories of her *pas de deux*.

Two Sisters

Nail Cousin Lettie's long dress
to the tabletop. Be quick.
With Mother's sewing shears,
cut away her rich black curls
about which Uncle brags
with his stinking breath.

Then we'll crawl under the bed
and eat the toy fruit
from her Easter hat,
the two of us laughing
as the hollow grapes
pop between our eyeteeth.

We'll just pretend a goblin came
sneaking in. She may be pretty,
but is so dumb, she'll say
it's true. They'll never know.
Come on, sister, let's do it now,
for we are pretty too.

Polka Dots

At the St. Louis Zoo cat show,
one of the lions reached out with his talons
and slapped the tamer's behind,
revealing white boxer shorts with red
polka dots. On our concrete seats
on the other side of the moat which
separated us from the scary scene,
Mom and I thought it had been planned,
so laughed. In the paper the next day,
a story appeared, telling of the man's
bravery, since he was uncertain how
the cats would react to the fresh scent.
At that distance, we could not see well
and now felt guilty for having snickered.
A boy of twelve, I became envious
when Mom took my older brother
to see the half-man & half-woman
at the county fair, while leaving me
to wait at the entrance. Dad, who had
been away in Korea defending us from
a menace, returned from his tour
and woke me on the cot on which
I'd slept since he left. I looked at his face
for signs of recent wounds and traces
of near death. I noticed for the first time
the blackness of his hair, the deep line
his nose made above his white teeth,
the sharp, stinging scent of his aftershave.

Horror Movie

I was the one who was supposed to be
brave when the camera slanted upward
and the long shadow slid into the room.
But my legs jumped onto a seat sticky
from spilled cokes and greasy popcorn,
as I screeched out loud and she just giggled.
I released her hand then, but beside me
her uninvited friend coyly urged me
to plant a warm kiss on two willing lips.
How I longed to kill everyone just like
the monster that shambled across the screen,
starting first with the nearby intruder.
I knew then I'd never call her back
and was certain they'd spend hours trying
to figure out why I never kissed her,
knew they'd squeal I screamed just like one of them
in the dark at the Saturday matinee.

Legend of Dracula

Seamless doors leading nowhere opened wide,
and a voice whispered, "Welcome, welcome, my son."

I blinked into the startling light,
waking in the realm of mother's perfume,
where I all but drowned in the burning scent.

In silence, ice cream arrived, stark vanilla,
stiff like the nurse's white uniform.

Hating how my throat ached,
I longed for the darkness of thick chocolate,
the way it mixed and oozed out of sight.

Father, grim king of my dream,
I didn't see till I reached my own bed.
"You'll be tasting your old blood
for weeks to come," he said.

Seeing is Believing

Seeing Is Believing

I watch descriptive narrative theater on TV,
a service for the blind. Two bodies
collide and kiss away—smack, smack!
Everything unfolds as described; I'm delighted.

Remember when father or mother read
stories, the worlds that unmelted behind
our eyelids. Even then we saw, formulating
our beliefs on what we already knew:

A world predicated in a dab of mercury.
I watch while I listen, captive to each scene.
There is no shrinking away. Blindness remains
for me a strange and unfathomable terrain.

In less they say there is more. Goose bumps
in the ears? The hue of wonder on the skin?
I wonder about wondering then, wonder
about the mystery of loss, the loss of mystery.

Truly, it is so: the blind lead the blind.
In the end even language will not resist.

The Fatty Acid Shuffle

I will live with arteries and veins unclogged,
pumping clean blood. From here out, it's chicken
that's been skinned and fish that's been broiled. Call me
Jack Sprat, if you like, and ridicule me
for slicing away the rind or wrinkling
my nose at the sight of turgid juices
seeping beneath the marble. But when you
come from your surgeon proclaiming the need
of a triple bypass or a pump, don't ask
me for my heartfelt sympathy. I've warned
you time and again: leave salads undressed
and avoid all white breads. Learn to fear fat,
to measure out life in grams, no more "eat,
drink, and be merry." That means no tippling.
Measure it out in small doses, savor
the flavor—without butter—*sans* salt.

Break Up

When I told her she was Plato
and I Socrates, she disagreed.
I tried to persuade her, but she
resisted and insisted my name
was David. I took a sip of wine,
remarking on its bitterness.
She said she found it sweet.
Behind her eyes, I spied another
form of truth, perhaps an absolute.
I wondered when she slipped
me the poison.

Rattler Lore

I catch them at the back of the head
and pin them down before chopping
them from their spindly spines.
I wear 'em for a belt till they wear out.
Then I get another. I like the smooth
feel of them, their sleek pattern.
Some say snakes hypnotize their victims
before they strike, that you don't feel
the venom it takes so fast. Me, I'm wary.
I never look 'em in the eyes, and always
carry me a Bowie knife to cut, then suck
out the poison. Be prepared,
that's my motto. Always be the one
that does the wearing, not the one worn.
My wife claims I treat her bad.
She says she'll get even someday.
I tell her I ain't no snake. She laughs,
then says, "That's what you say."

Buster Crabbe

I swim like Buster Crabbe, head held high out
of the water. Crawling through the past, I
long for new glory, life in the Foreign
Legion, sometime before the sand seeped in.

The Chalk Drawing

From the wooded place beyond, the woman might
walk, if she found it possible, along the spindly
token road and disappear into the region of
infinite speculation. But the eyes can't make
her move, so we must trace her suspended motion
and constantly conclude the trip at the one
appropriate place, where she stands now in dirty
smoke that rises in a stiff plume out of the bland,
vacant ground—there where a woman's undiscovered
dream smolders in a salver hidden in the flat
mound of rust-colored earth: see, this is how chalk
works, making the mind mock its own raw nudity.

Dangers in Window Shopping

In watery blue rows, swimmers raced across
the dozen TV screens looming like Cyclopses
along the long black wall of the H. H. Gregg
showroom—eye catchers. Like a fly seized
by a spider, I stood entranced among gleaming
appliances (radios, stoves, washers, dryers,
refrigerators), craning my neck. When
a salesman blocked my view, I stepped aside,
but not quickly enough. I was stuck there
like the living dead. Someone unseen
flipped a switch, bringing, as if on cue,
new pictures in a dazzling array, the better
to mesmerize the innocent. Numbly, I
mumbled lame excuses while trying to leave.
"Just looking," I stuttered at a beaming face
barely seeming to disguise its wistful leer.
As signs of life faded from it for an instant,
I careened toward the glass door. Exiting,
I saw reflected in glaring fluorescent light
evil disclosing itself, albeit, in reverse.

Outpatient Surgery

Thus the surgeon's steel scalpel scraped toward
my spine. Draped over a spongy pillow
like a picture of just shot pheasants,
I could slyly observe my doc's grubby
Reeboks and listen to his boom box
blaring out Dvorak. Music, he claimed,
helped him concentrate. So, in the sterile
room, with its cold light and clinking
clutter, my surgeon sang, happy
in his industry, while in blue-tissued
shoes, his nurses monitored vital signs
and passed syringes filled with novocaine.

With each succeeding squirt, my poor doc grew
angrier, admonishing me for laxity.
"It's far too deep," he said, "you shouldn't have
waited." Then he plucked out the offending
cyst and in disgust named it "plum," before
holding it, fat jewel, under my nose
in his now quiet hand. "Look here," he spat.
And I beheld the ex-lump in my back,
both relieved and afraid, expressing my
gratitude and hope to kneecaps and feet,
praying for the test results to turn out
right and more time to look, listen, and feel.
"Negative is good, positive is bad,"
the doc said, removing his mask. "We'll call."

Skunks Get Even

Squashed flat by truck tires in driving rain,
all that survives of it now is its slimy pelt,
flattened pancake-thin on slick black asphalt,
and the stench seeping through open vents
and bouncing around like crazed x-rays,
or brains sizzling like bacon in a greased pan.
Revenge is sweet, they claim. I'm not so sure.
Sometimes it stinks to high heaven.

After the Harvest

A mule dangling on the near side of the fence,
its neck outstretched, hooves hovering inches
above the grass they will never reach: we drive
past, mouths twisting open at its bulging eyes.

On the radio a song by a dead musician plays.
After the day comes night with its green
hues mirroring our own off-colored skin and
tiny puzzled faces that house another's sins.

We could call the Highway Department to verify
the vision of the big brown beast hanging like
a sack, but motion makes us want to keep quiet,
with only our radio's stories to keep us on track.

Spill

Unseen motorcyclists raged up
and down the beach in thick fog
until well after midnight. Basking
in phosphorescent light, sleek sea lions
lay atop flat rocks off the coast of
California bellowing news of fat
offspring. In a pickup camper shell
someplace else, two people who'd eaten
oily fish stayed. The man slept,
but the woman hunkered with a dog
named Elvis, smelling its spoiled fur
and missing her sharp scissors.
Next morning the truck's tires spun
in the sand before finding their grip.
In the back a dog whined and growled.

Crucifixes

Three giant crucifixes, blue, yellow,
iridescent red, point the way homeward
from Pennsylvania. On the mantel clay
gods sit, in the heavens men from mars.

The Carnival Elephant's Burial

They had to cut a hole in the parking
lot and dig the pit with bulldozers, so
Edith, the troupe's remaining elephant,
could perform the ceremony, pushing
Danielle's dark, slack bulk over the edge
to slide and then roll down the deep incline.
Dressed in rumpled khakis and smelling of
fresh hay and his own sweat, her old trainer
recalled how Danielle used to filch Edith's
fruit when her back was turned. Blended into
shadow, he longed for sudden, absolute
escape—cool rain, the sound of truck motors,
a florid place lacking all forms of gray,
the ability to forget all names.

Cloud Cover

Wallace Stevens women, large and buoyant,
scud into view, seeming pure. I close my
eyes and listen to them whisper the names
of certain men that dissolve in the strong
wind. When I look at them later, I think
they have changed, that they have become the sprites
nurtured by seafoam, mist become new clouds.
But they haven't; they are just girls of spring
that come flowing again, down again, to greet
us once the snows melt, and when we thaw out.

Among Mayan Myths
Mexico, 1989

Balancing on one leg while leaning
into hot Yucatan wind on a parapet
at the observatory in Chichen Itza,
I pretended to be the jaguar god,
ready for flight. In arms grown sinewy,
I carried you away from the pool
where virgins were sacrificed. We made
love early that night on a minuscule bed
in a pleasure boat bound for America.
For a moment, I thought of worn,
narrow steps winding upward inside
the tall temple, which countless travelers
tred now as then, amazed I'd never once
bumped my head. I took pride in the way
I kept my balance among the lurches
but more pleasure in the way you laughed
when I began to growl like a spotted cat.

Photo Opportunity
Paris, 1992

At the Place Madeleine, a dog and cat
sleep tucked together in a doll's bed.
Everybody stops, not just the tourists,
to observe the unlikely tryst. The organ
grinder, his beret doffed to accept change,
provides the background for the interlude.
Like the other voyeurs skirting the ancient
eglise, we take heart in the performance—
a brown dachshund and white Persian
lying nose to nose. They seem almost human.
Eventually, though, we tire of their snoozing,
and long for something different, and so
I deposit one silver coin before we drift
toward the *chocolaterie* and wine shop.
There as I stare through glass at rich, dark
squares laced with cognac, I find myself
recomposing the recent scene, but not
sure what to recall, and wishing now
I hadn't complained of the small weight
of the Japanese camera back at the hotel.

Rembrandt's Choice

In the foreground and in back, there's little
enough to see, suggestions of a field
in winter. Yet in the middle, the dog
hunches at the telltale angle from which
we normally want to avert our gaze.
Here it fascinates. The grizzled dog seems
noble, even wise, as he waits and waits.

Vietnam

Vietnam

In the movie version, the cutting is so quick
that everything goes by in a blur
like a bad acid trip. Green and yellow
splotches, guys zipped up in body
bags. Nobody survives. It lasts
two hours and a couple of minutes.
When you come out at the end, there's ice
on the parking lot, snow on the cars.
That was some movie, you think,
glad it never really happened. But
then you remember. You went, you lived.
Only the story came out different, because
here you are now counting your blessings.
When you were there, everything
was slow, crawling like smoke from
a grenade tossed to mark a landing zone.
When you were there, you weren't quite so old.
When you were there, you never really were.
You dreamed you were back home in the movies.

The Shop Teacher's Tale

Behind German lines, he and two others
lay under snow until the patrol passed.
Then they rose like ghosts to throttle and knife
the stragglers, leaving behind one of their
own, wounded and soon-to-be-dead. He still
remembers the pressure points he was taught
and can disable an unruly boy
with cool dispatch. "It's spooky," he says,
"because sometimes you don't want to quit."
When he goes in the woods, there are moments
he feels staying behind would not be so bad.
He naps in a tree's roots, shotgun cradled
in his arms. "You know what I mean, I know."
But I don't. I was in a different war.

The Homesick Patrol
II Corps, Republic of Vietnam, 1969

One of my fingers hooked into the belt
loop of the guy leading me to a place
on the green map—six numbers that marked our
spot. While fat mosquitoes waltzed in my sweat,
a bitch-moon watched me move with an evil
eye. Behind me my sergeant counted on
me to get him home, clinging close. He glued
his ear to the hissing black radio
and stuck his mouth to the mouthpiece, ready
to report. I was the lieutenant. So
I practiced coordinates, while like a blind
man, I followed our unfamiliar host
down a well-worn trail, praying for quiet
and to walk complete through the starry night.

Spooky

I'm sure the NVAs caught
in the great lantern light
don't feel they're in Hollywood.
More like rats scurrying
for holes, with none to be found.
I stay alone in a comm shack
ten klicks away, making sure
the spotlight doesn't stray.
We crave accuracy.
At dawn, the VNs will count
the newly dead. By mid-day,
the corpses will swell like ripe cheese.
Our hosts will hold their noses
and grin. We'll hold ours and grimace.
That's the cultural difference.
Listening to the hiss interruptus
on the squawk box, I resurrect
Marilyn as she walks across the grate,
exquisite and unobtainable,
a blast of air pushing up her full dress
exposing the purity of all that whiteness.
You take your Hollywood.
I'll take mine.

A No-Meat Day

Through mid-morning, the dead NVA,
with his characteristic big teeth
and broad face, lay still in the road dirt.
He'd soon begin to smell. While
his comrades had escaped, he'd raised
his head an extra inch to catch
the bullet which strayed into his brain.
He hadn't even time to blink.
The only American who could be spared,
I was sent to represent, and stood
to one side while two Victor Novembers
from District Headquarters laughed
and discussed, according to my interpreter,
the removal of his head. Why provide
an enemy with a happy afterlife? I wondered
if I should tell them the body, perhaps
from the warmth of the sun, was turning
waxen, his arms and legs green branches
and his fresh ochre and yellow uniform
the leaves of a plant created by Rousseau,
painter of paradises—vegetable matter.
The eyes, however, didn't or wouldn't change
and continued to stare at the sky, clueless.
When the truck arrived to pick up the remains,
the body resumed its almost human shape.
Quickly, I congratulated the friendlies again
before jumping into my jeep. If my luck held,
I figured I'd get back to camp by chow time,
already having decided what not to eat.

Space Odyssey

The NCOs didn't like sci-fi, anyway,
so didn't mind when the big guns began to bang.
When the new kid from Baton Rouge hit the deck,
he gave us old- and short-timers a real kick.
Once upon a time we didn't know incoming
from outgoing, so it reminded us of our innocence.
I remembered when I saw *2001* for the first time.
I was just a stoned-out kid, goggling
at apes trying to become men by cracking
skulls and learning ABCs. Man, now it
seemed liked old hat. Maybe I should try smack.
Then I might feel like stroking an obelisk
instead of my M-16 or flying toward Jupiter
instead of digging my foxhole a mile deep.
I called to the kid to turn the movie back on.
I wanted to see the end when the guy transcends.
Even if I couldn't live it, I could still pretend.

Not for Everyone

The Vietnamese lieutenant said
it was his brother, tired of war,
who had walked, already a ghost,
in front of their machine guns.
The American *cô-vàn* remembered
a story about a brash kid who'd
been drafted and died the same way
back in the World at Fort Bragg.
A friend had told him, "I couldn't
save him, and I can't save you, so
don't ask." He hadn't thought about
it till just now, realizing it had
never once occurred to him to beg.
He could tell from the handshake he
exchanged with his counterpart
that they both understood that this
kind of life was not for everyone.

The King and Queen of Siam

The woman who loved me for the six nights
and seven days claimed she was VC,
inviting me deep and deeper into her body.
When I spurted, I had fucked the enemy
and survived to brag. Smiling,
she told me she thought she resembled
the chimpanzees in the zoo. "My uncles
and aunts." The only picture I still have
(the camera with the film in it was stolen
at the airport) shows her hand
holding the foot of a male gibbon,
merely a cousin. We smoked strong weed
and risked capture by the MPs. I was never
in love, though I loved her dearly.
When I left her in the cab, she claimed
she was PG and would stay drunk
on the whiskey I left behind.
It was okay to butterfly her with a girl
back home. She wished me long life
and many healthy children. I kept the picture
of hand and foot in a plain cardboard box.
Sometimes I look. For a moment I am King
of Siam, she my most beauteous Queen.

Dead in Vietnam

When Grandma was dying,
I remember being told to stay in
the car while you went inside
with Grandpa. I stared at the
dark, hospital room window,
trying to understand a secret.
When she was being buried, you
told me to wait alone in the house.
When everybody got back
from the funeral, I wondered
why nobody spoke. What had I
done? When your dad died,
you did it again, deciding not
to distract me with the news
lest I grow too careless. Among
the dead in Vietnam, I might
have wept at least once. But, no,
you saved me from myself.

Rommel's Escape

Across the miles of desert sand,
you can see the enemy approach—
his name is Rommel. Anything
but scared, he rides in his Mercedes
in open sight. You wish you could
take a potshot, but accept your fate
as one who must watch and wait.
The general's troops, although clever,
are easily outmaneuvered and often
fried in tanks, no contest for the brave
screwy Americans. Knowing what
to expect, you marvel at how easily
a war can be won. Lately you've become
an addict, tuning in every night
to view each grainy episode. Too bad
they're all in plain black and white
and not the green jungles of Nam.
Too bad you didn't get to kill Rommel.

Camping Out in the Delta

Between the chirping of crickets
and the call of mate-seeking toads,
his unease develops epic proportions.
When he crawls into the sleeping bag
inside the pop-up tent he staked out
at twilight, he's afraid of sleep, not
because of bad dreams, but of what
he may discover in the morning when
he unzips the flap and crawls through
the portal. Next time, he'll sleep under
the stars, he decides, letting the light
blister behind his closed eyes to burn
away the memories that scar his mind.

Night Vision
Khanh Hoa Province, Republic of South Vietnam, 1969

Red tracers crisscross
the green ones, burning in after-images
that scar our tender synapses.

Back home—Cleveland is
superb, I've heard—
the Fourth burns bright,
all crackles and ka-booms.

There it's different; we watched dead-on.
Here we turn our faces to the side,
sliding along pathways and moving
among stark and uncertain shadows.

Our night vision must be protected.
Noises far away assure us
we're still alive. The close ones promise
unwelcome surprise. Darkness
tells us we may survive.

Back in Cleveland, July the Fourth
fizzles out, and people go home.
There we would sleep in beds.
Here we may only doze in our foxholes.

Replica

They got all 58,191 names on the copy,
even though it's half the size. At 250
feet long and six feet high, it's as black
as the original and should inspire awe
unless you are too tall or stand so close
that the sense of proportion is lost.
Here's a chance to pay homage to dead
or lost men without making a costly
trip. For memories, you can get a few
snapshots of the wife and kids against
the shiny surface. Or rub golden names
on thin paper. Who'll know the difference?
Perspective and a proper shutter are
all you need. And to take careful aim.

What Were You Doing?
April 30, 1975

When the end came, I was sitting in front
of my TV set, an old black and white,
in Lake Charles, Louisiana, drinking ice-cold
Jax beers and munching Doritos.
You couldn't eat just one. To me it seemed
exactly like when the Japanese bombed
Pearl Harbor on December 7th, 1941.
Even decades later, when I saw the wreckage
in old newsreels, I found it hard to believe,
but knew it had to be true. How could
we have been so stupid? I wanted to call
some of the guys from my old unit and tell
them to tune in. "You won't believe it,"
I'd say. But I believed, so why shouldn't they?
It was one of those days like when John Kennedy
was shot or they dropped the A-bomb on Japan.
I wanted to pretend it hadn't happened, but couldn't.
Or wouldn't. It was one of those days.

Just Like Fried Chicken

Just Like Fried Chicken
for Joy Scantlebury

At Les's bayou camp, we drank gimlets and basked in
the sunset. Joy said she liked to ride in his boat
and go out far enough to encounter dolphins. "They
have beautiful eyes when they come close to the side,
and their skin is so sleek. I like it when they talk,
although I can't understand a word." Joy brought
a fondue set, so we could try deep-fried alligator tail.
It might be illegal to kill one, but it was already dead.
Why not try some? Why not, I agreed.
We skewered meat so white it seemed to glisten
under the lamplight, then dipped it sizzling into hot oil.
It sounded like mad mosquitoes. "Maybe it needs
a batter?" Joy worried, the perfect hostess. By then
I'd drunk too many gimlets, made milky with gin
and Rose's lime juice, to know the difference or care.
We took out the meat, and it seemed to sigh
as if stepping from a hot bath. On the count of three,
we all took a bite, getting our first taste of reptile.
"What do you think?" Joy asked. Les said he thought
it was good. I said it was rich. Joy laughed, "I'm sorry,
and I don't know if it's me or the gimlets, but I think
it tastes just like fried chicken." Through the darkness,
I saw the smile in Joy's glimmering eyes, as if they stared
up from the depths of the sea. When I glanced through
that window, it seemed I saw the moon for the first time.

This Is About Betty, Who Died
Lake Charles, Louisiana, 1974-75

Telling me was as bad as if you had bared
your scarred and denuded chest. Not only
did I not want to look, I didn't want to hear.
(Your confession was not good for my soul.)
All I could think to say was a feeble sorry.
Then you said your bones were turning soft,
but that you would like to help me any way
you could. You needed to feel useful.
I demurred, and when you kept asking,
I said there was nothing. (What I wanted
was you to tell me you would not die
and would go back to teaching your class.)
You thanked me and said, "Don't forget me
if you need anything, anything at all." When I
didn't see you for a while, I was almost relieved.
(I didn't like to think of your becoming dead.
I'd seen enough of that to last a lifetime.)
One day I read about you in the paper. How
you'd drowned in the bath. Alone by yourself,
the family away. I saw your knees sticking up
like masts on a galleon. (Why hadn't you
jumped ship?) I imagined your form obscure
among rising and falling whitecaps, my leaden
arms tossing out a ringed lifeline. I could not
reach you and thought it improper to wave.
So I shouted against the wind, "I'll miss you, Betty."
I saw your face look back, hoping you heard.

At the Bamboo Club
for Larry L. Fontenot

Fluorescent blue flooded Katie's skin,
so it glistened like rich oil. She smiled our way,
not at me, at you, the white boy who played
lowdown blues on his Fender. "Oh, Katie
Webster, I love you," you crooned, groaning
like a schoolboy while her Hammond spooned.

How little we knew about what we would do
back then in the Bamboo Club, dark as night except
for the light from bar signs and what crept
from behind the band. On that night you warned
me, I remember, not to sound too Yankee if I
intended to escape alive. Anything, even death,
was possible. But we were alive and yearning.
"I want sex, " I screamed. You laughed out loud.

Sometimes I call you from across the country,
tiny amplifiers of sound held to ears and mouth.
We're like strangers, you the computer programmer,
me the paper pusher. You sound tinny, not good.
Last time I called, I bragged, "Hey, I found a Katie
Webster album on the Alligator label. It really cooks."
"No shit," you said, "please, won't you send it?"

Westward Ho!

in memory of Peter Van Dresser, El Rito, NM

Peter watched the skinny, bare-chested kid
ride his horse to fence and back, swaying high
above tall scrub grass. "He's stoned—plain useless,"
Peter said. To me the kid was playing cowboy,
his flapping bandanna a harmless flag.
I complained of a dry throat. "Water, please,"
I begged. "Fine. Just don't waste it, or I'll charge,"
Peter said, as we left his garden scraped
from hard flint and strolled back inside the dim
restaurant, the means of his livelihood.
"I'll have Coke instead," I said. Peter smiled,
and brought the bottle from behind the bar
along with a tall glass he'd filled with ice.
I smiled as the liquid fizzed and then gulped.
When Peter's good wife offered me a chance
to bathe, I was like an errant son, long
from home, feeling gratitude but weighed down
by guilt. It was one thing to acknowledge
the prophet, another to remain at
his elbow. Thus I left, smelling of sweat
and unclean, barely suppressing the urge
to wave to the profligate cowboy, who
like me longed for the wide open spaces
and also turned out to be no danged good.
Seated in my green Plymouth Satellite,
I tromped the gas pedal and headed out.

Shade of Blue
for J. B.

Behind closed eyelids, the color of blue
is like that painted on a doll's eyes,
and it sinks back into a place as remote
as distant mountains no one ever climbs,
except you, all alone, where you swim
in a mysterious lagoon that welcomes you
and only you. In my swimming pool,
paddling in water reflecting a cloudy sky,
I stretch out my open hand, pretending
for a moment that I have caught you.
But in the blink of an eye, you are lost.
In the blink of an eye, you are immersed,
porcelain surrounded by bright turquoise.

The Call of the Wild
for Jerry and Lou

Standing near Lou on Alaskan ice,
your 'copter gone, you marveled
while glacial ice cracked like gunfire
beneath your padded boots. Texans
to the core, I imagined you couldn't
help but yearn for fiery enchiladas
and tequila shots to make you warm.
Sweating on the beach in Mexico,
I sat beside Linda drinking *cervezas*
while she sipped *margaritas* the color
of lagoons. I remember I longed then
for something akin to an igloo. Later,
when we swapped tales, I imagined
myself circling above you in the air,
ready to swoop down and save you
from the cold. Jerry, when I spoke
about my sunburn, did you think
to provide a salve? Such are our
dangers, the only way we'll have them
now, thank God. So here's to you,
Jack London, who makes us catch
our breath, and here's to us, before
we all go our merry way to dust.

Absinthe

for Guitou Nanin

In those days, we copulated
with sea goddesses, believing
we could live forever too.

We would not end up
as Oscar Wilde had,
cadging drinks and misremembering.
Absinthe was our cloying nectar.

We watched for Brigitte Bardot,
our starlet of choice,
on the beach at St. Marc,
wanting to keep her to ourselves.

As a matter of course, we lived lives,
despite our greatest efforts to
remain uncorrupted by matter and time.

Beautiful, blonde BB tried to die,
sick of men wanting only to kiss her ass.
By the time she moved near an island,
she preferred the company of beasts.

You stay in Las Vegas,
cowboy with a French accent.
I live in Indiana, pretending
I'm some kind of exile.

They made absinthe illegal at last,
but I still lose my car keys and misplace my wallet.

Thanksgiving in New Orleans
for Bill, Janet, and Liz

To work off his mashed potatoes,
Bill told a story about the black mambo
he killed with a broom handle
in a swank island bungalow,
when he lived on the largesse
of a crazy New York patroness.

We liked the story, particularly
the part where he bought a spell
from a local witch to ward off evil.
Then he swam in the rich lady's pool,
ate lobster every day, and ogled
his girlfriend's nubile daughter,
till bored, he returned home
a vagabond in his native land.

Liz brought slices of pumpkin pie,
baked in a stove where mice
had thrived and left their funky odors.
Complaining of fullness, Bill refused
dessert, squinting into cigarette smoke
and drinking strong black coffee.

He promised one day he'd make sherry
crepes. Janet told us not to hold
our breaths; she hadn't even tasted them yet.
Bill grinned, watching as thick smoke
rings twirled up to the remote ceiling,
then oozed slowly into nothingness.

The Blue Buffalo Skull
in memory of Robert Sidnell

Back at the house, we took the skull
a deceased drawing teacher had used
to show the ins and outs of contour
onto the porch and hung it from
redwood rafters with kite strings
we'd passed through empty sockets.
Spraying on layer and layer of blue
from a can of paint Dan
had bought at Wal-Mart,
assured it was the color of daylight,
I acted as Dan's chosen acolyte,
performing an as-yet-undiscovered
ritual, while he urged me to cover
it inside and out, to make it perfect.
We did our work. I covered bone,
while Dan stood behind me, witness.
At last, when the paint was dry,
we cut the skull down and carried
it inside and placed it for a moment
on the yellow cover of a magazine.
Anxious for a new sun to display it in,
we drank whiskies and waited
for dawn, wondering silently
and aloud how the glossy skull,
now bluer than any known sky,
would appear and what strange,
unruly songs it might then sing.

Fire Sisters

in memory of Hiroshima and Nagasaki

They imagine us, when they gaze
on cherry blossoms, as two beautiful sisters
alive on snowy mountains. They do not think
of heat-white hearts shining among blood-red
stones, do not consider the fish in the streams
blackened in the spewing steam. No, for them
it is better that we remain two young girls
with smiles like sly geishas and laughter as shy
as hidden tears. We exist far away, lost among
beautiful clouds. They pray we'll find our way,
yet know we're better off where we are, playing
a kind of hide and seek, but never found.